This Other Life

PETER ROBINSON

This Other Life

CARCANET

ACKNOWLEDGEMENTS: These poems or their earlier versions have appeared in the following places: *Acumen, Aquarius, Critical Quarterly, Delta, Dragon, English, Fiction Magazine, Granta, Green River Review* (USA), *Infolio, Ink* (USA), *Lettera, Naked Masks, New Poetry 5, Other Poetry, Perfect Bound, Poetry Now* (BBC Radio 3), *Poetry Now, Poetry Wales; PN Review, Siting Fires, Stand, The North, The Trinity Review,* and *Twofold*. An earlier version of one poem appeared in *Overdrawn Account* (1980). A few are reprinted from *A Part of Rosemary Laxton* (1979) and the present volume reprints all of *Anaglypta* (1985).

I am indebted to the editors of all the above, but especially to John Welch of The Many Press. I would also like to thank Robert Jones, Marcus Perryman and Rosemary Laxton for their help in writing and completing this book.

First published in 1988 by
Carcanet Press Limited
208-212 Corn Exchange
Manchester M4 3BQ
and 198 Sixth Avenue
New York, NY 10013

British Library Cataloguing in Publication Data

Robinson, Peter,   *1953 Feb. 18-*
  This Other Life.
  I. Title
  821'.914   PR6068.0196/

  ISBN 0-85635-737-5

The publisher acknowledges financial assistance
from the Arts Council of Great Britain.

Typeset in 10pt Palatino by Bryan Williamson, Manchester
Printed in England by SRP Ltd., Exeter

Contents

I

II

III

ONE

A short history

Let me introduce first light
through gripping ivy round the window
which enlarges tendrils, leaf shadow,
telephone wires on the ceiling;
and my parents, waking tired,
struggle to rise in the next room;
a Sunday, to early communion,
hurried steps measure
a lot to distance, and restore.
Then, the service finished,
we make back through the city's
fringes, its vanished
forestation, wrinkled asphalt:
a drowsing land
where grass can reach waist height
on central reservations, sites
of motor industries'
loading bays no longer manned.
Desirable, second-hand
cars with ridiculous prices
pasted to windscreens
are found abandoned; advertised
clearance ripe for development seeds;
now the church roof's robbed of lead again.

Light condenses through massed cloud
above the aerodrome.
We follow straightened access roads
laid to lead you home,
where, in the stillness, dew forms.
A cargo plane's perched on the apron –
the wide embrace of its wings' arms.
Its adjusted ailerons
catch flame, as the sun's rays disclose
this industrial suburb
whose lace-curtained windows
are still undisturbed.

We waited under meshed stained-glass
on walking days, the parish limits
our route as light withdrew
from pre-fabs, flatlets, condemned terraces;
woven emblems ruffled, unfurled,
and their bearers staggered.
Gathered on the park,
(buffetted images at last unburdened)
uplifted faces dad addressed
from a lorry's back, speech amplified:
your authorised language
to reiterate certain promises,
father, outdistances
bounds still beaten with banners.

Reticulated power-lines
writhe above the wide boulevard,
where fast clouds briefly congregate.
On gift days, each year, coins
of the differing denominations
skim across a wooden plate
while you practise being grateful;
and, vicar, for small earthly reward,
worry over this pastoral
care – your decanted parishioners,
the damp rot and dry rot
in floorboards, roof timbers,
or squat church tower's
dilapidation fund.

                    Your calling
filled the house with "God" and "Hell"
and flaming words from under doors,
a whisper of insistent voices,
phrases drawn from thin air:
incumbent, gratuity, burnt offering.
A herring I took from the quay-side
the family ate with guilty relish.
Fingers smelt of soap and fish.
Bricked-up chapels of rest, the tombs

bear spray-gunned additions
over deeply engraved
tributes to loves, and separations.
That little extra earned from funerals
or the Easter bonuses,
dad, the making sacrifices,
you know what it is to want money.
There were sides-to-middled sheets
through years of being canny.
Forgetful and repentant, mother,
a small mend in one of your gloves,
writing held family together:
us, edgy people growing apart
with each of the subsequent moves,
and stray notes that commemorate
how you've made ends meet.

Granny, after Chardin

A suggestion of summery clouds
at Seahouses, beyond the harbour wall
where, expecting, you were knitting
baby-clothes for your third,
in a light cotton dress, with neat bun,
and the line of shade under your sun-hat
intimates a plump face contour
in impassive profile –

I suppose you couldn't move your head
during the exposure, neither smile
nor speak, till your possessive husband
took the photograph,
which later emerged from fixing trays
(in his darkroom we children
were forbidden to enter)
as finely differentiated greys.

Hinted-at sorrows, the ructions
surviving relatives recollect
for my benefit; but alone
before your picture in the quiet room
their ruminations vanish
like the sound of needles clicking.
"Peace at any price" was how you lived
and now you have it, perfect.

7 October 1982

The earthly remains

Late getting started, we were last
in that day's funereal routine
and, inevitably separated,
granny's hearse was caught between
delivery vans as she journeyed past
changed façades of various take-aways,
a surviving cinema, the library
I borrowed from on family holidays,
dilapidated churches where she worshipped.
Nobody saluted, or gave way for us;
and shoppers, in fact, hardly noticed
our broken up, mundane procession.

By the finish, she'd felt caught in
her exhausted body, which the four men
could quite comfortably carry.
That portable burden of her sin
she left behind; and the worry
of caring for her, like so much dust
collecting about their home,
remains with the relatives encamped around
uneasily, as dutiful acts they just
didn't find time for, recollected now.
Some have wandered off alone,
or they sit out vigils in an alcove window.

Loose from a handbag, the family album
had curiously given up its ghosts.
A few last words of comfort, then
curtains of the crematorium
closed with their automatic ease.
Dewy eyelashes, tendered handkerchiefs –
you find near relatives, unprepared
for her dying, are consumed
with guilts that wouldn't burn
or lift, remorsefully make amends
and sandwiches, for afterwards,
when we ate up every crumb.

Under their feet

1

Once the remaining great-aunts had gone
I walked where granny carried us
on early holidays; watched a trawler, homing,
pitch between embracing piers:
domestic lights were coming on
in flats above the North Tyne
fish dock, and fishing lines
tautening under a vanished horizon.

Their seaside resort seems that empty,
closed – "as if it had been sold,
but the new owners not yet moved in."
Shiny black mermaids hold
marble torches to the night; my feet
edge round cleared borders in South Marine Park;
shadows, insubstantially complete,
fatten the shrubberies with fears of mine.

For only too late to speak with her alive –
their well parked cars outside –
half-estranged relatives finally arrive
to a clothes rack lowered by pulleys
from the ceiling, brown patterned linoleum,
tub and mangle in her scullery,
deeds, newspapers: all their things
had grown decrepit round them.

2

Last night, in bedrooms shadows stirred.
Before dawn sleepless bereaved heard
under my feet a staircase groan.
Searched by white revolving rays
from North Pier's beacon, walls
flickered an instant like a film of drifters,
colliers, lifeboats sketched on holidays
– then were as skittishly gone.

I saw that dressing gown, silver hair
in a long plait down her spine,
how she'd encourage us with jigsaws
or, where the North Sea foamed against them,
pointed out dock-gate remnants
that slipped tug-moorings in a storm,
irretrievable – as her memory
for faces, and sense of time became...

Not in her regular church, our last hymn
faltered beneath its ribbed nave.
The young incumbent called her
a legendary figure of the Mothers' Union.
That saint's stained-glass shield
had been pierced by a vandal's stone.
Would she ever have believed
those doses of tears, or her daughters' valium?

3

Here drifting has buried the long-laid paths
through dunes; there's concrete slab
for seawall repairs, unfinished amenities...
What brings me now to understand
why this disappointed place
has a look dead relatives' years
of expectations, aftermaths
insinuate – all at once resilient and drab?

Remember how coarse grass had taken hold
on the roof of that locked air-raid shelter?
Stubble of wrought-iron railings
in low walls we balanced on
still unrepaired? Our parents' World War
was over but not done with –
the air my questions breathed.
And you must have been about eight years old.

Shut out of our grandparents' quietened home
behind its stark privet, for being too loud,
we'd found cover on that roof nearby
reconnoitring how to break back in
while pleasure craft exhausted their bought time.
Nursing my anger, with bare-faced shame,
I promised we would be less heard.
You asked to be forgiven and allowed.

4

Out of the flaked brick wall a single frond
sprouts in mortar; where steps ascend
graffiti survive what loves they name.
A laden freighter unbinds the sky and sea.
Though carried from a muddled youth
with people that we couldn't choose
but be attached to, and would lose,
I'm borne back to ourselves by grandma's death.

Nothing recompenses for the love withdrawn –
as if I'm unsure they'll ever let us back in.
Yet other histories beyond our own
intermingle round this shoreline
where Tynemouth Priory grips its headland:
an ebbed tide's stinking wrack
of seaweed and sewage, crude oil,
children's stick drawings score wrinkled sand.

The family would shelter behind stone ballast
on this beach when we were young.
Though, shuffling off into darkness
damaged footprints disappear,
where enclaves were demolished
alleyways still cut through,
and, unforgiven, comes home to you,
the pieced-together past in which we did belong?

16

5

Back home, mum's relatives speak their mind
uneasily, close, with such conviction
and head of feeling uncontained.
Surely not foreseeing contradiction –
these near strangers in a half-circle
round the black and white television
defend themselves aggressively; they heckle
outsmarting phrases, expressed views not their own.

Beyond drawn curtains, inward rushes
of breakers are pestering seashore.
On the sofa, I see dad wishes
he hadn't ears to let him hear.
Only speechless, a family's choked griefs
heated behind eyes and cheeks –
bear that in mind, beyond others' beliefs –
and not to mention art, or death, or politics...

After a quiet life

1

Recalled at last, our survivor of Gallipoli –
an under-age recruit for seaborne assaults
on the Ottoman Empire – seriously
wounded in the shoulder, sides, and front
when mortar bombs brought to a halt
their progress for ever in that trench,
he was piled amongst the agonies, sent
painfully slowly to a forward clearing station
with stretcher-bearers sickened by the stench
– not knowing, he wrote, which way to turn.

Returned here to a lifetime of service
on the Martin's Bank cash counter,
he was well used to the touch of every coin
for more than ten years now not legal tender:
smooth profiles of bearded kings, their value
declined with his savings; yet he was true
to "make do and mend", "look after the pence",
a model of politeness to all his clients
but taciturn, short when at home.

The pieces of metal lodged still inside him
gave little trouble, but disarmed us.
All those bitter winters he had nursed her,
his one love, and then outlived granny.
He'd say "You've a tongue in your head",
though quite beyond me how I speak
as he leant by the fireplace, wiry, slight,
well-preserved on what one great-aunt said
had been a spartan diet –

I asked him "How are you?" He answered "Canny."

2

Grandmother's dark-stained upright –
I nearly remember her playing
– wouldn't even sustain
half an echo of the testing duets
with his polished violin
arthritis finally silenced.

Then a generation's rumours
in the air, through years unmoved,
blamed him for their long-held rest,
saying it was he forbid
her old reopened scores
and the concord locked under that lid.

A proud isolated man, it seems
he'd found that difficult to bear
being disturbed by others' pleasure;
but, where no music resounds,
left me these few words
disenchanting inert furniture.

Yet still you'd hear it resonate
while I've tried to recover
a tune contained in us we missed,
though with the spent lives to justify
who can tell it did exist
now all sound's hushed for ever?

472 Claremont Road

"Poetry 'is capable of saving us,' he says;
it is like saying that the wall-paper will
save us when the walls have crumbled."

In the house where my father was born and grew
– tattered lace flapping from a broken window
in its dereliction – wallpaper was fragile
as I brushed against it; then
anaglypta, the word is, hung on while
brick or plaster, whatever the thing was,
gave to my touch: like digestive biscuit
crumbled under packaging.

Restive in the faith that has sustained you,
I hesitated down the high, narrow vestibule –
her threshold, at which I was to kiss
your mother's loose-skinned face,
its poor textures; but the cheekbone's hard
curve was there, enduring years too ill-defined
to recover, quite plainly, for not a soul
emerges out of inner darkness.

Try and see once more the buried features
wrinkle in a front door's frosted glass.
Overleap gaps, the cracks in her yard's
paving slabs chalked out for hop-scotch,
mocking omissions. Glance backwards;
but bound to lose your musty, obscure
interior with relatives about the range fire,
how little may be saved – to my mind –

papering over its faults, were that the word.

In my father's house

By the vicarage fireside, you were trying
– mother, as I read the paper –
to anticipate fears
of homelessness and widowhood
in a living room never your own,
made familiar all this time
with oddments on what-nots:
ballast of the tied accommodation.

Childless, as if you were once more,
days extending before you
waste the past years
of bearing and rearing us,
parish work you'd been subdued to:
effortful the while to be
reliably good-natured
against your temperament and moods.

Long after, the palsy that had frozen
half your face
petrifies again the twisted look;
and informed by an eye that cannot blink
or shut, I'm not sure
if it slurs your words as a mute rebuke
to us, cold at the windows,
where a squat church tower
intrudes on the featureless air,
stirring an emptiness which is of a piece
with the depleted horizon.

Plain money

To my father nursing a drink near midnight
as he stares at the wall and beyond drawn curtains
– Dad, what's out there in the darkness
where the gasworks was? A by-pass
abandoning your parish in its hollow,
tail lights streaming elsewhere. Do you know:
is it worse to be corrupted by too little
or too much? Where does money go?

Entrusted with an errand – you remember –
greedy for distant places, I had spent
mum's change on foreign stamps: meshed grilles
with padlocks and a brisk ringing till
shut tightly. Lying to evade repayment,
I said I'd dropped her money in the street
where, doubtless unbelieving, she had sent me
back into the dusk to find it.

Whatever was thus lost, I'd not recover
there on Bootle's pavements, eyes cast down;
yet framing stories, wandered over
far as Johnson's Dyeworks once again.
Not to return without it, this was plain –
I'd have to go back home and make repentance,
but passing outside the Pacific Hotel – saw
a pool of someone's sick dried on the floor –

which marked how near he'd reached towards its door.

Faith in the city

1

The white seagulls dip for scraps above
Long Lane's central reservation; brittle leaves
are ousted by heaped shreds of paper
and, at a football pitch's edge,
I'd watch a while the Sunday League game,
clouds and my father's parish in its hollow;
now across those pieces
of a swallowed industrial village, I know
I shan't reach a destination –
for avenues proliferate
taunting each approach, crossroads appear,
beyond a cutting and the railway station
distances congeal, it's late
and front doors shut
– or be an equal of the animated faces
who pass by, indifferent here.

2

The photographs of a lifetime's service
were about us, seeing them, there
in colour on the mantelpiece
or, earlier, in black and white –
my baptism amongst them – and it's quite true
I'd soon enough be driven away
from mum as a child, portrayed in the frame,
leave you in this vicarage
with consequences, unforeseen,
to live with, can I say: a shame
and guilty feeling, inner rage
which would have had to find its voice?

3

I imagine you now, accelerating your car
across a depleted horizon of the city
with gasholder surviving
and a church by daylight –
all the unspeakable between us
like debts I've carried far,
as if another were to tell me –
I forgive you, yes, but will you change?
No, you won't, will you. You are what you are.

TWO
(1975-1985)

There again

1

Our witnesses were just visible views,
mountains north-west of Milan,
as lightning flashes at four in the morning
revealed taut power-lines,
and by crash barriers, puddled verges
encroached on hard shoulder;
a cloud burst dissolving the distances
softened reddish clay earth,
the predictable returns of windscreen wipers
like mitigating circumstances.

2

Yet seeing the muzzle of an automatic weapon,
(his other hand fumbling
with your tricky brooch) I nearly relive
the taste sour breath has
harsh against your expressionless face,
and the unutterable humbling
my being there couldn't relieve.

3

Driven into a landscape without choices –
where no law was applicable
but his common sense's
wanting an object, you would serve.
And wait was all I had to do.
Because the first thing's to survive,
you said you'd bear the consequences,
whatever he demanded, giving me
occasion to revise or think again
how in that lay-by, and alive,
we viewed each other differently.

A trial

Through the yellowed marble halls
of the Tribunale di Milano
to where behind judges' heads a Cain and Abel
wrestled muddily on the wall,
they ushered me – a witness to corroborate
your suspected innocence –
for the court required that I state
if we'd received a payment –
and you were called to describe the gun,
how he turned from his windscreen
threatening, forced us
to let the thing happen
which their young interpreter,
a woman grown embarrassed,
had stumbled on... Needed no longer,
relieved, then given our expenses,
we'd stepped down into clear January air.

But in the lobby, where everyone waited
until the accused had been brought in chains,
his lame wife was haranguing us.
This, though untranslated,
you could understand.

Outside, while you gave evidence,
she repeated her complaint
to maybe journalists or advocates
that were standing round.

They'd been trying to appease her.
One of them asked was I your husband.
– No, il fidanzato della ragazza,
as he would explain.

From a memory

The cypresses were disordered
by sharp gusts; bedraggled strands
flurried at your face beside me.

Extenuating circumstances
for my part towards him,
I blame then am uncomprehending.

Vain regret comes back to mind
and, in the petrol station's bar,
chrome shadow, you shivering wet.

Dolls in plastic bags, soft toys
for souvenirs hung where you said
– I concentrated on his tie.

Yet now you swelter in the dusk,
are chasing flies, abstractedly,
until you just forget them.

Darting at the part raised shutter,
they blur into the contre-jour:
that pink blank of a wall.

A September night

Come to bed late, I'm quiet
    across floorboards, hear
uneven spattering rain beat
    on rhododendron leaves,

you breathing, the whirr
    and click of a set alarm.
Unsettling shapes recur
    in sleeplessness. It's two a.m.

Shadow on a nightdress
    softening creases, touches forms:
the hollows where eyelids press,
    or down along your forearms.

Tonight's not warm. And waking
    you wrap round the counterpane.
– Windscreen wiper blades making
    sweeps at sheeting rain,

the livid dark enfolded us.
    Soaking in that downpour,
drenched embankment grass,
    you lay still there

and for a little died.
    And I don't comprehend
your sleep like death to settle
    or arouse you –

I'd just make amends.

The harm

Fat moths rub their bellies
on our bedroom window's lighted glass;
irrefusably, disparate pasts
are summoned from this night's cloudy mauve...
Sometimes putting my lips to yours, I have
a daunted sense of other lovers
pressing to be near, as from that flat upstairs
our neighbour's girl's short cries
and her breathing we'd just bear.
The rhythm their movements would make
carried through single brickwork:
clearly pleasing each other – long
and loud sighs – his imperatives awoke
your distanced hurt, incorporated wrong.

Cleaning

Seeing as she submerges
disturbances of the foamy water,
unnoticed here, I look at her

skin suffused with warmth, the margins
of her self and I acknowledge
urges he pressed home, my fears.

Lathering reaches of her front
to punish in herself another's want
and be clean, she is fierce;

roughly imagined by him;
taken as though insubstantial;
dispossessed, possessed – my victim.

Unannounced, I lightly touch
her streaming upper arm to speak.
Only it startles her so much

an overfaint quiet is thickening.
My mistake, never reckoning
how still you are afraid of me

or my imagination. Being
not specially alone, alive I'm
far from the person who endured him.

My love, this is the dirty thing.

Vacant possession

Ourselves locked out again, I glare
into where your kitchen was
at correspondence, circulars,
and then the telephone rings.

Bare, these entire walls are
untouched by any proprietary sense
of him or her, removed furniture,
the various pieces that hold a glance.

So this is your vacant possession:
those few rooms filled with air.
Uncurtained, jammed sash windows
let onto sandtex beyond the front door.

Caught by the sunlight, pink goosepimples
stand out of reach like poor examples;
you're keeping to yourself, withdrawn
a distance inside thin skin.

Hopeful, nonetheless, you plan;
though builders couldn't promise how
soon ease should materialise
obliquely from that stippled shadow,
I'm keeping my proximity.

Soles have muddied floorboards; faint
odours in unmoved air remain
and one barely visible, ghosted hand-print
smears an uncleaned frosted glass pane.

For Lavinia

When she re-entered – from mutilation, rape
– unspeaking in a painted Roman landscape,
I couldn't rid my own mind of those shapes...
for you had also stared and strayed and cried

without a sound, besides the wind through trees,
rain on the road; what could I ever say to ease
your unfathomable hurt, now each turned phrase
unnerves – as bad weather does dumb scars,

the shame she's not permitted to outlive?
It dries my tongue and lips till they can't move.
And what would I be trying to achieve?

Lavinia, I've said too much already.

THREE

Early territory

Caught sight of, ground mist wafts
after rainy spells across the Stray,
or from allotments smoke drifts
and Belle Vue Terrace looking the same
though, to us, it conceivably was –
its dead-end the rusty locked gate
to this wilderness.
        Shame-faced yet
at self-deceiving explanations
for motives others must have seen through,
unforgiving, I conjure that time
from the close afternoon, a stickiness
even to the breeze that fans late
blushes; lupins in full bloom
stir between headstones and grasses
pollinating.
        The vast, smutted mausoleum
with its cypresses dilapidates.
For earthly reasons, prolonging them,
I'm wanting again to disinter
a self mostly thought better dead.
Disinterestedly looking for –
you've not the least idea – someone
absorbed in taking down particulars
from mildewed, slant tombstones
restores me, unnoticed, to the day's
chance composition.
        Here, compounded
by a cloudless false limit, strong
sun exposes cool perfidious
tinglings of my own skin; but, whereas
short-cuts still twist through,
now just you confront me, reckoning
the years' uncalculated wrong.

Landscaping near Heslington

Ducks awoke us with their mocking laughter
and half-tame geese take flight
if I encroach; it was unlike
me, at first not reminded in these environs
of myself by leaves overlapping water – despite
how little's altered, to mistake
its views, come back to them years after,
amongst protected species, though no swans.

Convenient, the covered walks that skirt
this artificial lake
drew towards us, seen afar, ashaming faces
studiously unavoidable; my heart
barely in them, the sickening distances
covered not comprehending ourselves, our senses
of one another twisted with sharp phrases
bluntly turned, for your or my or nobody's sake.

The lengths we went to, mutually compromised
associations have further
dispersed lapsing friends from those days –
us, who could not keep faith with our pasts.
Rare birds feed from my table. Their loud
feathers flex in short migrations. You couldn't know
if things should have been any other
who this would be, restless to make some last

telling remark, so tenuously long drawn out now.

Depending on the weather
for Carol Friend

On the road to your hospital through worsening rain
again I have misjudged the weather,
am sheltering from it in a chance bus shelter,
body lengthways on the bench,
and the edge of damp over paving slabs
where droplets leap would inch
by inch encroach on me.

Others, cocooned in the music of their cars,
splash past half oblivious
and pedestrians, cyclists, more hardy
or less vain, push on regardless,
drenched in the quickening downpour and thick spray.

Out of it, I think of how, balanced on the margins
of our lives that long ago
we paced the Fulford golf course, taking lines
to talk other people's differences away
or – forestalling fears –
whatever would become of us.

Ten years on now, you have had two children,
complications: the necessity
you sensed for them, had taken pains
explaining also that to me...

Underneath the weather front, glistening final sun
has slanted through close trees,
globules of rain water on their steady leaves.
Though I've turned back, visiting hours almost over,
as a rainbow forms
above the changing traffic lights, anxieties
evaporate, all goes fine for you –

me cheered by the oldest illusion in the sky.

For different friends

Bestiaries, crowned heads, statues
populating the sky
and, above gateways, mottoes
just intelligibly applied
to their memorial stones
without the ghost of a problem,
unlike our day-long conversations,
being in awe of them
as we crossed indisputable ground;
layers of the unimpressed
clouds raised their backs above the town
and others as rapidly dispersed.

Those times I had to speak to someone,
fretted by disturbing
words' drifts still being absorbed –
so that troubling friends
if bright self-possession's gone
my limits were extended
by various examples, tracks
through the evening's
picked out frozen solid marks
of bicycles, feet – familiar things.

Walking then amongst the trees'
angular, elongated
branches' shadows cast like arteries,
I appreciated
the pausing unemphatic breath
of another speaking;
only now to leave beneath
those clouds of my own making.

Bay Hotel

It is out of season –
                    no one
occupies the corporation benches
with their cast-iron serpents
supporting the planks. No couples.
And it's late in the day
to be yourself. My lungs expel air.
A bulbous church hall radiator
giving some heat, the sash window
gives onto an aspect of the shore
between two headlands. I asked for that
on the telephone, but sit
with my eyes fixed on the beds' feet,
grey interview suit in the wardrobe,
toothbrush under the mirror,
while seagulls and pigeons compete
for a scrap.
                Their cries get through to me;
I understand that we receive
but what we give, a paying guest
shifting toward sleep now at last.
Wind disturbs the barge-board
of a bandstand shut up for ever.
Down the front, barred clouds at dusk
retained their acid pinks though sun
had almost gone: a chorus line of sky.
My lids are closed. The next days
shape up to compromise
between settling down, and getting on.
Waves' habituating repetition
exhausts itself. Inertial pull
grates on the shingle, pressures
of some future scraping by.

Temporary poems

1

Loud breakers expend their force
against the promenade.
They suck back, hurl pebbles
at protective shutters
of hotels' windows and front doors
long since fastened for the night.
But to touch on our department's troubles
– that locked office of a man
with some incurable disease –
"He's not coming back," you'd said
for the company. "I wish he would
push off," his fill-in muttered at the sea's
alarming foam columns,
"At least then I'd know where I stood."

It's past half one. A solitary woman
leans on the sea wall's
stone parapet, absorbed by each long
withdrawn rattle; her eyes
turn towards quick spray
rising at irregular intervals,
which punctuates talk. "I realise
my callousness," at length he said,
"his death near certain, interminable,
still, I've my future to watch."
"It's a pain," you had to say
now from the shelter of a lit porch
as we separate into darkness
and the pattering rain.

2

The temporary gravestone of his office door
offering us that little consolation

seals up an evacuated room...
He is not here; but as others are

(colleagues wanting him still to have lived)
no one's removed yet this sign he existed.

It will soon enough flake his name –
the post being frozen – like any mildewed tomb.

"That the axe must fall is not in doubt,"
acquaintances confided, "I'm just holding on."

Still, with the homesickness of someone
as at home now as anywhere, my gazes fix

on the borough's permanent caravan site
settling into the hillside. Envy it,

or that he gave in peacefully at home here.
The wastage is natural, he dying young.

Nobody could tempt you with the run-down front.
Facing redundancies, they may only warn

of no prospects from this elevation.
And don't expect to be here long.

3

There was small coin from a cold fish's mouth
to weigh, as tribute for his service,
hopes unaccomplished and only the truth.
How hard it is to show promise:

each of us being what we do, more or less.
Within the year, they discover his talent
buried under earth: a windfall that was
to crackle a while and be spent.

I found myself fishing for compliments;
remain with the threatened, alive
to reassurances everybody wants
(but which this sea front couldn't give –

only wave curves foaming at the headland,
that bitter far end of the promenade)
and to think of him being beyond
praise, the criticisms, or reward.

By the lines

1

Whatever there is to be said, let it be
in the form these leaves have giving shade
to a wide, concealed footpath
at the base of flaked walling; beneath
their tendered protection, each stride
recovers ground where I had made
repeated short journeys, examples of words
which have shaped and feed me.

*

This area's car maintenance enthusiasts
cannibalise for spares
the gutted bodies of family cars.
A scavenged engine leaks its sump oil
while attention is lavished
on moving parts. Windscreen fragments
glint over paving: the essence of a thing
quite spirited away – a quiet spot,
the curb, though not much left there lasts.

*

These mute summer mornings' activities
subside; yet gently stirring trees,
best roses of the year
trail spider's webs – mist particles
bringing to light their tenuous
sticky threads whole days let disappear.
Now, killed last night by a passing car,
that suburban fox's carcass
has swollen, stinking, to become
a talking point, a disposal problem.

2

Insinuating buried lives
murmurs of a frothing stream
reach here through grilled manhole covers.
Lines sing just as a train arrives.

Clinging to wire mesh interstices
ivy in-filled with the litter
this summer forms a solid wall.
But there are interruptions, humming aftermaths.
At twenty to or twenty past the hour
as Southern Region services go by,
the leaves seem to cower
shaken by suddenly turbulent air;
flashes and sparks underneath each coach
from the broken contacts
leap across live gaps to touch.
And I can't stay here –
on account of the monthly cheque,
the self-respect that keeps us dear,
love pressures us apart.
Your eyes glued to that kitchen window
repeated along the façade
in similar developments, see row after row
of plates on draining boards drying,
imagine a happiness somewhere near.

In silence broken by the scores
called from tennis courts after trains go,
I hear the noise of waters
under my feet distinctly flow.

Towards Twyford, 23 March 1985

Against the current,
curious, a cygnet on the river Itchen
steers itself beside reed beds, the greasy clay
and chalk path I have slithered on, whose grey
mud's spattering these ruffled townee clothes.
Unmindfully alone, it nears through easing rain:
an enviable creature, protected, in its element.

There's the last fleck
of a faint brown on its folded wing feathers
and articulate yet still scrawny neck,
which twists now it hisses to intimidate me
– me raising my head towards where the others
have noticed I'm not with them, and they turn
to find me staring risibly at that almost swan.

It drifts my way
a moment with the water's motion, then resists
the quickening stream; but I continue –
a mistiness seeping from the watermeadow,
as if you'd glanced out, during an interview,
and seen beyond their office window
vistas of the not-to-be just snatched away.

Hackney Marshes

for John Welch

Commuters read on platforms, still,
the second I glanced from your book
to pale bright February morning sunshine –
preoccupied lives caught in dazzling haze;

and paused a while on the railway bridge
which you pass under every weekday,
I woke from a doze to the silence
of this train's last empty carriage.

Tall reed grasses' tufted heads
waver with the mildest turbulences;
waterfowl, waddling against clear sky
on a reservoir's embankment, baldly gaze

at flats and a patterned stone church spire,
parish streets whose narrow slots of azure
open onto threatened common land.
Along rear walls of factories, in the wars

of white grievances, unspeakable graffiti,
painted out at least once, reoccur.
Not the muteness of a language classroom
nor when, between kindnesses on the phone,

speech falters, and, at the end of the line,
no one takes it up – here, in a warm
suffused light where I can imagine
you pacing towards work, a moment's peace

before words – the silence breathes and forms.

An impossibility

In a difficult July, this evening, peace
and stillness find me
by the weir's loud agitated surface
speculating over depths
beyond the drop; then gone
on to meet an almost stranger
I must say goodbye to,
past rings of pale wood sunk in grass:
the elms' memorials.
Composed, this steady alternation
of sunlight and tree-shadow
across the curving path before me
stretches out beyond the sense
of any obligation;
recumbent in cool meadowsweet
are close-cropped sheep
whose hearts rapidly beat,
myself and others here given to see
in the life about you
their own phantasmal presences.

As leaves' reflections reach up to me
their drowned veins,
the points of sight and touch revive.
Though at first alarmed
by your impulsive invitations,
in an open face's trust
I've found myself reformed.
And the park's green wedges
hold their distance;
the quivering stalks, close foliage
give ground now I accept them –
grateful for the fact
and moments of reflection
within these daily postponements of a life.

Editorial footnote

"This window will see us out."
Adrian Stokes

Shown into a dark panelled study room
on the second floor, his things
the same you could imagine: handsome
pottery, and figurative paintings.

Bare wires marred a wall; the window
view that saw him out excerpted trees
in hierophantic attitudes and now
upholding still life objects. "Please

find within unfinished drafts, last proofs."
That utter quietness of someone else's house
absorbing street noise, roofs
attached frontage to sky – a loose

grip that had released his life.
I stumbled on details, the slight depression
in a chair cover, still as if
he had just risen to leave and gone.

After the explosion, 1654

Broodily still, the seller of musical
instruments thumbs a trim beard;
under the awning of his stall
a signature vivifies encrusted wood.
C. FABRITIVS, like the lute's bowl
your canal turn swelled, the ground tone
bringing touches of autumn to trees round
the new church; a viol-da-gamba's f-hole
curving counter to the cobbled street,
taut strings above a sounding board
pitched to the bridge, and these few words
held off from the near unearthly quiet.

In painted ears, inaudible cries
and appalled, fellow townspeople
carry makeshift stretchers: a pupil,
the sitter, two relatives from the debris
of his collapsed house. Dull spires
point up a louring, powdery grey pall
in innumerable copies. (His family portrait's ashes
flew out of Rotterdam's fires.)
Trees are stripped, and a few birds veer
over rough sketched figures who bear
with no small difficulty from his view
a dying painter with singed eyelashes.

All conventional or extravagant praise –
"the greatest Delft or Holland had known,
worst damage suffered by the town
soon made good" in Bon's poem, the gallery's
peacefulness; so close my breath
condenses there, I'm looking on as if
in delicate touches were choked griefs.
At your first wife's and children's deaths
ten years before, my musings start
where speculation also finishes:
shiftless clouds tinged with varnish
in the surviving piece of art.

51

FOUR

Feeding the dead is necessary

At watery dusk now you park the car,
not one outboard, no windsurfers
disturb the flat calm of Lake Garda

which released distinguished vocables,
a noise like moist lips smacking.
Our time ripples beyond us, disparate

stretches of the given landscape.
Low sun glances off the cloud banks'
illusive headlands; reluctantly

you mentioned what occurred here,
saying, "We can't reach the dead,"
and I agreed with you, "to touch them,

or, still more, renounce them."
Sweaty currencies of daylight, making
alloy glint in every wavelet,

render up indebtedness, and peace
now the harbour is abandoned
for the bar's television set –

a championship of Europe fought
between old, natural adversaries:
these recent friends. And quietened,

disquieting emotions not that far
from petrol spillage, moored dinghies
belly barely noticeable swell;
rumour each present, remote war.

A summer thunderstorm

Eating ice cream on a terrace at dusk,
above the lake's ant-ridden edge, confused
amongst the cypresses – that vacancy
where the water was – though bounded
by villa window glints on the far shore,
a paddle steamer's fancy lights gone by,
as dance music floated on the dark to us
we heard it intermingling our talk,
moving with the pleasure craft; we saw
leaves tremor, felt air pressure drop.
Far off lightning flashes came closer,
flatly reprinted mountain peaks. And though,
night chillier, faint rain spots struck,
we sat out there till we were sure.

He showed all his dog teeth when he spoke,
our host, still spinning out his locality's
bloodied past: that means of execution
by flinging from ramparts onto stakes;
private quarrels settled without the law
when violence held towns, and the nation;
it had been an evening for brutalities.
Water thrumming on the shuttered panes,
into not remotely vicious air, a skein
of propensities to hurt and war
teased out again, I talked in turn
of shop displays looted, uprootedness, how
a district of my home town burned
in civil disturbances some nights ago.

1981

Overlooking Verona

Had the gate attendant tried to cheat us
by short-changing, I wouldn't know –
my hold on the currency too precarious.

But I felt you tense in that shuttered quiet
where niched figures eyed us; we'd to go
the length of their blind, nearby street.

In an arbour's shade you had appeared calm
seeing a hill-slope smudged with olives,
and attended to our postcards home.

It's being foreign to this style of garden,
seeing the differences that gives
vividness to not much out of the ordinary.

Yet I too started at a satyr's mouth
– grotesque, in stone, debouching clear
water from amidst thick undergrowth.

Breathless, irritable, sweating hard
we climbed the height of a belvedere:
there stretched painted bleached façades,

the traffic's exhalations, high rise
offices, red striped chimneys, campanili
grating dusty blurred horizon...

Still these could not be yours, for you –
made nothing from them – must tell me,
"I prefer moisture, greenness, shadow."

Sunshine's irresistibly ravished all the view.

English as a foreign language

Morning once more, your English Language School
has its grille shut fast.
Where smoky flames of two oil lamps
beacon a taped-off hole
the tarmac of this stunted road subsides.
An excavator stranded in the meadow
raised those mounds of dust
to make foundations, but for what I don't know.

Concrete fence-posts with rusty coiled barbed wire
delineate a barrack area.
And yet there's no end to defensiveness.
Convent walls, hill forts define
the city's outskirts, its snow-filled precipices
not in sight, as early mist
has drawn a limit beyond the last
suburban halts along your autobus line.

– As if the world stopped there, my teacher friend says.
Outlines of townships, final cypresses
hold their ground against the shifting haze.
Further talk touches absurd
discountings of the heart, obligations to save face.
Terraced olive groves, my guesses
at the unforeseen grow tangible
now I understand the meaning of a new word.

News abroad

for Tim Dooley

On a bench by the statue of Cavour
just before Easter, we were sheltered from the glare.
The kiosks were prophesying war
half-intelligibly, and I'd hurried from square to square
after an English newspaper,
but without any luck; so the thumbed dictionary
justified itself once more
providing us with "resignation",
"requisitioning", and "put to sea".
A mild breeze was lifting palm branches
down the waterfront drive,
rustling our paper like a comprehension test;
and, as then in exam rooms, anxieties
gave way to blank incomprehension.
We paraphrased wishfully, wildly guessed.

Forewarned, as I approached them,
seagulls would rise from the flags in close formation,
souls of the deceased that swoop and glide
or haunt the sterns of ships.
Before us, shifting on its anchor
as we rested by the dockside,
the distant profile of a laden supertanker
vanished of a sudden into lowering mist:
and the skyline still there yet we couldn't make it out –
news staying news though I don't understand.

1982

Towards darkness

to Vittorio Sereni

Through suburbs, flooded meadows
beyond Milan the train curves
at dusk; caught in carriage windows
a red sun bobs above telephone cables:
one of those nervous dots
that settled an instant on syllables
as we sang at the minors' matinees,
watching in a partial darkness
usherettes with ice cream trays
aim torches at the sweets and coin;
my father's and grandfathers' wars
played out – I refought them
in imagination and the overrun
vicarage garden, grown aware
through that quiet of my absurdity.
And at the cinema, one Saturday,
mocking the action, I spoiled
for a bruising from those others near.

As if they were invidious, askance
eyes turned upon me or mine
envying that man's scope, the glints
of electric engines' smoked rays shine,
make visible Turin's terminus
blacked out by a power failure;
vast shadows circumvent barriers,
ghosting refreshment bar penumbras.
Bruised on my tongue, their rumourous
language, like an almost closed book,
lightens weighed-down baggage
of touchiness, things, anthologies.
With your gratitude and reticence,
through obscured exits, guide me
further than exchanged stilted phrases,
before you enter the collected dark –
I have barely begun, and the work
so soon leads into silence.

At Salò

1

Because of an oppressive silence
still in that fine late September weather
or, conceivably, others'
scars borne under our own skin,

they'd both not wanted to go;
but strolling past city-registered cars
and postcard stalls, we saw
through transparent altering water,

broken outlined, on the shallow floor,
a rowing boat moored to a jetty
had foundered in the swell
which flowed away from this side

– the stillness outlasting all wars,
you'd thought, but, dreaming the Republic,
that were they to stay in his city
the poets should be collaborators.

2

And on walls of an empty pizzeria
colour covers of the *Corriere*'s
illustrated supplement
showed exploits of their boys in Eritrea...

Comfortable couples on the lake front,
its forty intervening years
hadn't managed to efface
how through the months their remnants tried
to cleanse the stain in blood,
that picked out lifelines as it dried
on a disembodied hand –
snatching out towards us
from where we'd failed to find
in desultory corners any plaque or trace.

3

A veteran wearing the green forage cap
shuffled from an arch's shadow
as we drove away.
I glimpsed him for that second
like last fragments of an atmosphere:
in the lake water's bits of broken mirror,
you were keeping yourself from yourself
and, guided by an interior light
above the warring factions
– from being overmuch aware
of the emptiness in their rule of terror.

4

Though more than once you came
for a bed, a bowl of soup, a microphone
where gunmen would tread on the dream,
across Lake Garda's silvered expanses
in still lasting peace –
impalpable light, its blinding waves
a dazzled refraction of ourselves –
it was as if you'd never been here.

Nearly in the clouds

1

In Emilia-Romagna, resilient sun
keeping us warm still,
illicit mushroom gatherers through the woods
we wondered which were poison –

had found some which seemed good
erupted through the coverlet of leaves...
Concealing tops and edges
in your Apennines, a ridge

of cloud dropped rapidly over fir trees
toward the picnic spot you'd chosen.
Tinkling bells in the air told me
cattle somewhere near had come

down before chill drifts and swirls
that promised to engulf us –
but held off; above the generous
spread of food, and father's wine,

they were swarming like an invitation.

2

Replete amongst its remnants –
your sister dozed off near, my wife
left us alone – exuberance
in English you had spoken
has found a way under my skin,
or on some nerve.

Walking further where cloud hung
through pungent-shadowed pine,
I was lost myself a moment
in diet, biology, love –
(you assuming the moon's influence
on your body) tempted –
and couldn't help agreeing.

But we were in her foreign country,
speaking little, and the bonds
of a life-deep familiarity
had seemed to loosen in the absence
of familiar words, or things;
above a chapel door she'd showed us,
on scales in the tympanum
souls first lost were heavier and dropped
to be raised: the light would rise
yet fell – a conceivable outcome,
and it makes the more sense
if she were unaware –
sweet figments, barren regret
accumulating in me
at the thought of my imaginary affair.

Aria di Parma

Over shuttered frontages and nearly empty streets the moon
rises into Parma's sky.
Night of earliest October – unusually warm,
evidently tremulous with fugitive temptations –
lets friends talk and stray under cavernous church baroque
left unrestored, almost in ruins –
at the tangled very end of confused, confusing youth.

Trolley-bus cables divide that deep blue, all but black –
redouble the street-lamps' glare.
Even though the torrent's dry and should be,
virtually every truth to tell, or compliment pay,
insinuates more torment in the name of clarity.
Surely still it won't unravel, though the waning moon
and dark have been surpassed by morning's obvious daylight –
now – on another couple's wedding day.

Leaving Parma

1

– It's going to rain soon, very hard.
Droplets of moisture in the air
appeared condensing on our faces.
At first I thought the trolley-buses'
power-lines illumined for an instant
strips of night sky between apartment blocks,
not the forked and sheet lightning it was
accompanied us through her streets
crammed with dark interiors of cars
from which eyes shone, where thin pavements
dense with intent, expensive features
impeded our having some last word.

Yet undeterred, she vividly related
how once in the mountains when a storm
imposed its thunderheads above them,
she'd lain on a groundsheet under polythene,
gazed up into releasing cloud
and electric flashes through the atmosphere:
immune to obscured impulses, elated
by lightning which had pressed
its acid flare on her recumbent form.

But as we drove away it broke on us.
Feeling safe behind the screen
whose wiper-blades were overwhelmed
at each return by flooding rain,
I was drawn on through that darkness,
vague shapes of a blurred countryside –
its petrol stations' still bright reminders
of the danger I'd been unprepared for
those ten years back – and I saw –

in his rear-view mirror, my insufficient fear.

2

Be that as it may, we'd stopped too long
over spontaneously offered macaroni
and the wine talking; though he'd rung
we left it too late, arriving in Verona,
my infatuation expounded as dark deepened,
to return her that loaned car
which might have been the living end
for his blonde Italian, burdened with her
family griefs, his near lost girlfriend
who the next morning had gone to her mother.
"And you'd been so absorbed you couldn't see
beyond your own dilemmas any other."

Across those bridges he had led me,
through pits of shadow between the lamps
along the Lungadige; unsteady
Vespas' beams down alleys stamped
his silhouette against the brightness.
If I'd thought myself exempt
from criticism here how wrong I was
(the daunting statue in Piazza Dante,
its down-turned mouth unalterably cross)
brought back to entanglements by my stay –
me not wanting to let things drop –
so that in the end he'd just have to say.

At the Fontanina

What momentarily stopped your breath
as we were talking, I don't know,
in that same restaurant where he'd eaten
with us one night four years ago.
Above our heads green-painted pergolas,
laden with ivy and wild vine
stencilled out against night sky
through wire-netting intertwined,
gave some support: for us –
just now distracted gratefully
by the dinner-table noises
of ragazzi enduring their military service,
that nervous camaraderie
– the place still overshadowed by his death.

What about the others'? – you'd correct me,
but are saying nothing, while the moon
makes itself known above Verona's
baked tile roofs, railed balconies;
already with one segment gone,
it faintly indicates the sloping shoulders,
absorbed head turning aside
of this attentive listener,
my friend, who'd led me here
with two languages through filled evening streets
and narrow warmth of bars,
to where I'm sitting opposite
a profile – inviting you to speak
in the hope that you'll explain it to me soon.

Their late effects

1

The stiffly carved-out oak furniture
and an atmosphere difficult to breathe,
this awkwardly intimate family picture
    you're uncomfortable with;

have complained of a wasted afternoon,
"It's as if I knew what days were for,"
of being left too much on your own.
    These things detached, unsure –

a life of saving, lost through one bad loan
– seem temporary, vulnerable defences
against the blank of their lately known,
    straitened circumstances.

In houses of about the last century's end
blinds are raised to the freshening breeze,
reveal red marble knotted columns and
    crenellated balconies.

This ceiling has a rustic chandelier.
It hangs on, oppressively low overhead.
Beneath your breath, though I still hear,
"I want to die...because I've no idea
    how to live," you said.

2

Through reddish bark of cherry trees
    a mistiness in the damp air
forms about the clutches of branches
    distinctly, blue haloes.

"She would have to bear responsibilities,"
    he'd translated involved stages
for me, where foliate house frontages
    rest in place, the last word.

It's beyond us to repair the errors
     her broken father made;
individuate each tortuous harm
     of mistaken loyalties;

summarize, or talk away her loss
     to show protectiveness –
as I speculate, here, on a bus
     in motion, yellow,

underneath the cherry trees.

A difficult passage

"Perché, oltre ad avere un corpo uno sguardo
e una voce, non siamo dotati di una speciale
trasparenza che permetta ai vicini di convivere
pienamente con noi senza ricorso a quella
distorta emanazione di noi che è lo scrivere
e a cui regolarmente li rimandiamo?"
Vittorio Sereni

1

White dust-covers shrouded the armchairs.
Her portable set, put anywhere,
emanated its grey apparitions –
mouths dubbed with foreign tones

but mis-matched gestures, disconcerting
– as we must have seemed to her,
with our spoken English, starting
to ease the senses from his lines.

The wrung-out thesaurus might serve
for well tried words, but, stymied by turns
of phrase or our interpretations
between what to compose and yet preserve,

you asked for the advice
of this blonde Italian with red hairgrips
and butterfly earrings: her softness,
morbidezza. I followed the lips,

puzzled at your conceivable faces –
as if you could like spirits embrace,
mix totally, a union of pure with pure
desiring, and be amid the furniture

a moving absence in the space of things.

71

2

Because there are the difficulties to love,
and late again it dawned on me
what you must have talked of,
made intimate with the transparency

or future, how he wanted "a direct
instantaneous emanation of ourselves,
undistorted, not delaying, in the strict
correlation of our acts and words".

Those versions of ours meant to respect
resisted his meaning: surely death.
Houseplants' air-roots reached out still.
As one in our bafflement, from beneath

his fretted-over words we could sense
a something of its own will
move our silence and stopped breath,
stretch towards us like a hand –
us half persuaded his tangible absence

would have been borne back from beyond.

3

Though the day thins, this much survives
of us, that January dusk, her Burmese
cat she'd driven through the night to save:
its body wasted by a slow disease.

Across the dialogue he had believed in,
a dead man seemed to touch us through the hum
and murmur of his tentative lines.
Yet re-united, here, we have become

ourselves the apparitions – presences
facing each other above chess-pieces
and dictionaries, snatching occasional glances
at her ghosted set. Once three readable faces,

we met, were overshadowed, and would pass
for ever from the curve of that darkening glass.

FIVE

Writing on the quiet

The things we said today,
I work on, at the window.
Curtain gaps, red tiled ledges
and the frame segment
odd, bright packages.

At their intimate limits
close frontage is absorbing
a woman by her open stairs.
And all you see is what appears,
she didn't put them there.

Drawn out across the grass
to where lit flats occur,
she writes a careful letter
railing at the noises,
her too hollow ear.

I'm discovered in a semblance
of composure, but the quiet's
made of many voices.
That silence is a vacuum
and taunts you into it.

Unable to alleviate
this being on my own
and you'll be breathing
evenly now, uninterrupted,
gone to bed hours ago.

Dirty language

"He would sit impassive at the window;
lodged behind the cream cloth covers
of somebody or other's Collected Works,
    would appear unmoved.

His time is dirt. Unrinsed empties
fill work surfaces, the tear-off calendar
    a week or so too thick.

It isn't you that worries me; it's what
    you do to things.

If he would wash his thinning haircut
in the basin, no, once there he'll only
    watch himself grow old.

And it falls to me to disentangle
hairs from the sink plug, stuck
to my soap so firmly you would think
    he hoarded them.

In the cabinet mirror, I see decay
proliferates from the face. Beneath it,
    silver paper wrinkles.

Collecting dust like dirty language, crumbs,
the mug rings, toilet wall inscriptions:
    the so and so was here.

Now it reaches everywhere. The days
trickle on to lino like a waterfall.
Sun sets for him at the window,
    when I close the curtains.

By artificial light, the darkness, this
    swells out of all proportion.

I polish the kettle, tarnished as
the word he uses, until my distorted
    features show through.

It makes no difference what I say."

In our own time

Soaping beakers at an alcove window,
her face obscured, lit from behind
she brooded on the outer dusk
that wells up over roof tiles,
turning then to talk.
You have no time for me, she says.
I bite but cannot swallow – words
with not a thing against me –
what I used to look for in them
now I start to fear.
Small birds fill out the quiet
with *a little bit of bread and no cheese.*
Responding to the pressure of a mind
lips make words no one's to hear.
Last light flashes on the weathervane.
This flickering in the glass,
it's a flag interrupting acute rays.
The brass hands of the clock
jerk round its dial, a sun, the roman
numerals gold above an azure disc.
Baked brick and sandstone of Lloyd's Bank
in shadow the lighter clouds sustain
and I look blank.
                    I think,
she was telling me of her difficult week
and it is too late for apologies.
About this loaned interior
headroom and the library impress
these phrases on my retina:
"You know as well as I do"
or "You can't pretend,
young man, you do not understand".
In all my life with her
I hardly comprehend her more.
She neither differs nor agrees.
Within the silence, each assumes

problems not to be deferred.
Time passes between us
pressing words, makes room
for the days' anomalies.

What the matter could be

From the chair you occupied
a moment ago, this winter avenue
of pollarded lime-trees
slips away beyond black keys
that my fingers hover over.

Leaky guttering, greenish slate
jut to the window where I look
bothered, taken with the crack
and chip in one enamel tile
which promises, withholds.

– It's you leaving these environs
stand in for, still composed
of things that cast a shadow
on me watching you go:
our life to be continued.

Splayed, fine branches
push from the limes' stumps.
Responsive, I have grafted
what was missed on past work
cut back, lacking you.

The noises of a sentence
faltering... this pretext
presses down poised hands,
then rummages my head for
what I am saying now.

Against the loss you make provision

Fringes of your shadow in the dusk
are diverging from my own.
A table's set between these forearms
and the climate of your features
– uneasy ghosts of rented homes.

Beneath the sloping wired glass
which graphs clouds' shifting light,
we swallow incidents and food:
our own lawn's unevennesses
grown when we weren't looking.

That desiring to possess our lives –
we barely lived; as night extends
a distance between us,
not far, the look in your eye
asks, What do you make of me?

We do not own the thing we are.
Against walls your family name
reverberates: brought home,
a self neither mine to have
nor yours for you to give.

Touching you

Sun on the dirty window pane
makes flecks of dust
and grease marks shine
with qualities I've taken from her,
waking in a frame of brightness,
rush of the words in her ear.
But she'll find no change
in the sky, as if the cloud
parts to let gold coins
of daylight tumble in her lap.

Then I'll be at the door,
a shopper with the week's provisions.
The differences you have effected
in me, narratives
of our bank statements
we could share... forgotten years
and the debts to be accounted for.
Put yourself beside mine, tell me
if the calm I've settled into
is my own or borrowed only.

Building society

Dark in between the blades of grass
before snow falls, night brings

shadows and a chill of its own.
Knowing how much I owe you,

who could spend a lifetime
or make a living at the window?

If they won't lend against your income
we remain here: expired ideas,

breath out of cold mouths.
The quiet has been furnished;

familial, an argument turns,
with chairs arranged to take up sides.

Corridors and concreted yards
for independence, but the hard

opinions settle in, preferred.
A blacker tree against the skyline

shakes above some pavement corner:
there insistence hesitates.

1979

For my wife to be

There was the odd impediment:
establishing where things went
and once collected, cleared.
Then in the rooms prepared

for renovation, whose debris
showed us how we used to be:
engaged, the habitual dissolves.
And we notice in ourselves

restored, the interior blanknesses
still to be cluttered, causes
of an eight-year hesitation.
After wallpaper had gone,

plaster used for messages
by previous workmen, passages
of four inch brick proved rough.
Here was relief enough:

our vertical bodies' residence.
Only love is small defence.
All you have I have to share.
What each gives, they are.

Home improvements

Streetlight at the curtain gap –
caked walls adrift and softening –
alternatives I had kept open
reoccur. What follows? Small hours
against the black lamp base.

You make choices, regardless,
then show me the improvements.
I gaze in through unnetted glass
to an empty front room, and kitchen,
and look for internal repairs.

Figure out the ground plan, your ideas,
the finite number of meals we'll eat.
A routine, care your features reaffirm;
on one side, I wait for April
when blossom and the monies come.

The sky is difficult

Ambitious removal man
or talking to myself again
in private grounds: the scene
a discarded pamphlet
opens in the conduit.

Freezing water turns
loose pages and softens
its manipulated senses
of a world whose bald existence
is deferred – coincidences.

A sunny cloud nudges
above the carriageway,
the straggled and disintegrating
expectations, not to be
frustrated or confirmed.

And my head fills with interior
rough furniture, an index of names
where the misquoted dead
argue with my friends,
the one idea discounted.

Looking up

Then where the daylight settles
adhesively, its brightness
mingles with the breakfast things
which are egg and coffee cups,
pared apples, a wedge of bread.
The shopping, correspondence, bills
reassemble in possible series
and a weighted apple bough.
This place no longer
those inventories of objects
which used to depress me, you said.

And the small room for despair,
her eyes fixed on a patch of wall
just to the left of me, anywhere.
For among so much uncertainty
there are no questions. Cloud tails
flake above early white sheets
and they come to resemble one another.
It's the plain familiarity
of each of them looks puzzling.
A polythene black question mark
bucks on lines beyond the roofs.
There were no answers, but no problem.
Variously the cirrus have refused them.

Change of place

Seedy grass sprung from the cracks
in a tile path I helped to lay,
again tread down; and all looks
well: the garden wildly prosperous
with tumbled over hollyhocks,
yet conceived in other terms by us.

Admitted, the shadowy crampedness
of a scullery she could hardly bear
entering ghosts this dining area;
now too the pregnant girlfriend
that we sheltered here
through morning sickness and recovery
confronts my too complacent care;
frayed, love vexed them to no end
of troubles, but I wept at the very idea
of kindness – a mockery
of my emptied gesture, killing time
in retrospect, as no one told me.

Stained floorboarding has mellowed,
though underneath the same
dead dust we swept and choked in.
This pitch of a wired glass roof
graphs still other ponderous
hopes for gladness, as our own have
passed on with the clouds that rear
behind a cockerel weather vane
rusted solid on its spire.

Ointment, floss, my things
temporarily hold the basin rim.
Back then, I shared the bathroom
with a flecked moth afloat in the pan
drowned by those outpourings;
now make myself a home
where happiness is a possession
we did not have the ease to own.

Thinking again

Out loud, as our chain-wheels turned
along the sticky road frequented
by gnat swarms or flocks, you yearned
for a change and whatever we wanted
was all the conversation.

         When I braked
to have seen the abbey ruin's architraves,
stone columns unsupporting – spokes
of sunlight, irradiated through turning leaves,
were shaded in by risen woodsmoke
and, mating airborne, dragonflies.

– "I can't think of anything more idyllic."
An Englishwoman's well-bred phrase
carried to us from shallows of a lake
exceptional circumstances, our holiday's
unburdenings, become blurred memories.

Drawn differently together, being loved,
had fed in me your quietened wish
for a change of place, to keep alive –
baulked by stippled, bleared whitewash
against us here – a frond of clinging ivy

trapped inside, underneath this window-sash.

A holiday's end

Beside the steep avenue of mausoleums
were picnickers, acres of tombs.
Inscriptions command
complete strangers to pray for us.
Resting places for those who pause
to catch their breath, the famous dead
manifestly aren't here –
others, monumentally unremembered.
Tended jam-jars bloom in the dust.
Wreaths whose laurels rotted and sank,
stay behind like skeletal life-belts.
Headstones have tumbled into disrepair.
Hisses of a grave-cleaner's jet
rebounding against stained marble,
its fine spray rising and dropping in plumes,
augment the mundane quiet
of lunching office staff, bereaved people,
and, amongst tourists,
us reaching our holiday's last afternoon.

Tomorrow, you return to case histories
of the terminally ill.
Controlling pain, their end comes soon
or soon after, suffered by relations.
Here the dead ignore us,
keep quiet about agonies, bliss or remorse,
but for laid-out voices, a composed verse,
silently wrenched quotations.
A part of this late summer morning's calm,
we're speaking to appease them.
You say you're fond, as I am,
of a cemetery's preserve, have found
a latitude of thought, affirmed limits,
as those widowers, and widows,
with employees of the city council
trying its air and ground.

South Parade

1

Tempters of incoming spray
scamper up this shingle beach
smartly, happily out of the sea's reach.
Down the tide's serrated line,
dusk come, their shadows stretch.

At low water, submarine
obstructions – not meant to cause alarm,
not long ago protective –
re-emerge, and arm in arm
our friends leave us behind.

Under foot the pebbles grind
ruffling an outspread calm,
while confused allegiances
surfaced again on your mind
repossess the worsening silences.

2

A Spithead Fort, that one of five monuments
to another invasion scare,
glints out in the Solent –
object of a once groundless fear.

Green slimed blocks agitate cold swell
forming at them; its war
not to occur, such peaceable
images of us we hardly were
remain disconcertingly as hard to ignore.

3

Ogee arches of this pier's arcade
are picked out with fluorescent strip;
lemon-drop bulbs, reilluminating,
write "Amusements" in a cursive script.

At its talent competition, to strains
of standards interpreted for different lives,
ageing couples staidly dance
on the fringes of a pensioners'
Bank Holiday outing audience.

The half affected voice half pretends
to be another singer's, entertains
hopes like ours, our disappointments,
which lazy music neither judges nor forgives.

4

All the length of Southsea's esplanade
the visitors in parked cars slept.

At quaysides – you explained –
on balconies, here, flags draped

and servicemen's girlfriends
lifted bared breasts, unashamedly wept.

Relatives, bystanders waved warm hands
at silhouettes in the late spring.

Around the lake, protected swans
lay down sleek heads on folded wings.

Coloured lights' flounces dip
between lamp posts: glitterings

shiver innumerably on wave-tops
– waves out of scale

with the bobbing model ships
smelling of their lubricants and fuel.

5

After the carriers and frigates left
– a few eroded wooden piles
protruding from the drift,
and reiterated lost appeals
evoking the drowned, with seaside
refreshment kiosks making pale
sad reflections in the tide –
you breathed again; but beyond
the ocean, other airs, and a wide
skyline, relations depend
(as holiday-makers straggle the prom)
on what in the world you imagined
we were edging towards, or away from.

6

Across an unmanned housing estate
named after military successes,
flickering, the lights accentuate
not yet closed accesses.

The dockyard, its hey-day gone,
is briefly reprieved from more losses:
public money's not to be withdrawn,
engineering opportunities.

Low sun returned by glass panes
of bus shelters: flaring opposite us,
the ornamental paving stones
turn faintly luminous,

until, its colour drained, this vista
flattens into far sharper contrasts
with what goes then may be missed
or, staying, wastes.

7

Yet gleaming strips of pale bark
on a garden's silver birch
stand out against long shadows cast
across warm, emptied beach;
still flurried, much darker
sycamores, these stuccoed guest-houses
with undermined foundations
(while two couples made their way back
and the sunset lasted)
move through sure relations.

1982

These last days

Amongst the clutter of subsided stones,
carved petrified ivy on a pillar stump
for our remembrance,
stopped still before this monument's
cut legend, as it says,
let a *reader be ready* in the sense
that though we'll be dispersed
others shall live
or the earth I enter
promptly does survive.

Smoked by the graveyard's small bonfire
of light rubbish, pruned branches
and dead flowers
we walk to the ornamental gardens,
then out along the esplanade
where illuminated fountains, working,
dampen paving slabs, and shrubs,
spume forced into bushes
by onshore wind to lean against
competing with the rain.

*

By the pier emporia's sheltered places,
as snuffling dogs advance
and the dogs' owner passes us
wordlessly, she says the quietening
thing again, a fretful qualm
at the decorative light bulbs'
blurred extremities, precarious calm –
as if each shadow had her body
in its vacant eye, I speak to comprehend
my wariness in a municipal park
given over to dense coverts,
muttering, the ordinary dark.

94

In the small hours

Starting from my nightmare
with a muffled yelp, relief
it was to become again aware

of you awoken by me, my own wife
perturbed at that unrest.
Dozing off, mercifully safe,

I remembered the half-focused
sunken, cowled visage
of death, the specialist,

stared into while trying to allege,
through barbs he'd reiterate,
my innocence of the charge –

slandering a Warsaw Pact state.

*

Block floor and ceiling mute,
unease gels in the chilly room.
At liberty, she is late

returning; through the still home
(bookcase, armchair, carpets
curtained from worrysome

car doors, shouts in the street
which reach near) a clock's too
loud ticking reverberates.

Released by the hour, that cuckoo
flies from its rusticated hut
mechanically, shrilly mocks you

just once. And settled quiet
which I should think benign
reasserted – yet this is what

her dying might seem like, or mine.

23 January 1980

My apology condenses on the window;
a new moon shouldering the pole star
above backyards that overlook
cypresses and ash,
resilience, the marble headboards
in the cemetery, and my fear
of not getting to sleep or ever waking
coughs like a stalling car.

As the earth grows colder, discontented,
under the winters of money and the freezing
of relations, how we live
matters less than this reflection,
that we continue
poorer or in health, and letters arrive
bearing affection or disaffection,
starting with, How are you?

Back home, what it is to be forgiven.
Close, I wonder what my furred tongue's for
as words to be uttered when she woke
my teeth close on,
and what should become of us
in the promises of further histories
I'm not asked to explain,
only to say no more.